Let's Get Cooking and with Coffee

Sweet and Savory Recipes for Caffeine- Lovers Everywhere!

BY

Christina Tosch

Copyright 2021 Christina Tosch

Copyright Notes

This Book may not be reproduced, in part or in whole, without explicit permission and agreement by the Author by any means. This includes but is not limited to print, electronic media, scanning, photocopying or file sharing.

The Author has made every effort to ensure accuracy of information in the Book but assumes no responsibility should personal or commercial damage arise in the case of misinterpretation or misunderstanding. All suggestions, instructions and guidelines expressed in the Book are meant for informational purposes only, and the Reader assumes any and all risk when following said information.

Table of Contents

Introduction 6

Breakfast and Brunch 8

    Cappuccino French Toast with Coffee Cream 9

    Cheddar Polenta with Sausage and Red Eye Gravy 12

    Chili Mocha Cupcakes 15

    Chocolate Coffee-Kick Granola 18

    Coffee Buttermilk Pancakes 21

    Coffee Glazed Brown Sugar Bacon 24

    Coffee Nut Loaf 26

    Coffee Oatmeal 29

    Macchiato Muffins 31

    Red Eye Eggs Benedict 34

Lite Bites and Mains 37

    Asian-Style Pork Ribs with Coffee BBQ Sauce 38

    Baked Cod with Coffee Butter 41

    Beef Chili with Coffee 43

Beef Fillet with Café Au Lait Sauce 46

Chicken Coffee Curry 49

Coffee-Brined Chicken Drumsticks 52

Coffee Coconut Shrimp 55

Coffee Crusted Lamb 57

Coffee Marinated Sirloin Steak 60

Coffee Red Lentil Soup 63

Coffee-Rubbed Salmon with Orange Salsa 66

Coffee-Rubbed Pork Tenderloin with Espresso-Honey Glace 69

Dark Roast Coffee-Infused Risotto 72

French Onion and Coffee Soup 74

Italian Cheese, Breaded Chicken with Coffee Penne 77

Mexican Turkey Mole with Espresso Coffee 81

Rigatoni with Coffee Spiced Pork and Beef Sausage 85

Roasted Espresso Coffee Chipotle Shrimp 88

Spicy Coffee-Baked Sweet Potatoes 90

Sweet Potato, Kale, and Ham Hash with Maple Syrup Red-Eye Gravy 93

Sweet Treats & Desserts 96

Boozy Irish Cream Frosted Coffee Cupcakes 97

Cappuccino Muffins 100

Choco-Coffee Covered Strawberries 103

Coffee Custard Tart 105

Coffee Mousse Rice Pudding 108

Dalgona-Style Cinnamon Coffee Brûlée 110

Date and Coffee Scones 112

Italian Prune Plums in Brandied Coffee Syrup 115

Mocha Cheesecake 117

Sweet Egg White Omelet with Chocolate Coffee Yogurt 119

Author's Afterthoughts 121

About the Author 122

Introduction

What do Red Hot Chili Peppers, Humble Pie, Otis Redding, Bob Dylan, Blur, Johnny Cash, and Frank Sinatra all have in common? They all sang about coffee, of course!

If coffee is your favorite go-to beverage of choice, here is some more coffee trivia for all caffeine-lovers out there.

- Brazil produces around 30 percent of the world's
- The Fins consume the most coffee worldwide.
- Coffee contains antioxidants that can help protect against diseases. So the good news is, consumed responsibly; it's good for you!

- National Coffee Day takes place every year on September 29th. A great way to celebrate this day is by cooking and baking with coffee.
- The only coffee-growing state in the USA is Hawaii.
- In 1511 Mecca banned coffee, believing it to stimulate idleness and radical thinking.
- Adding coffee to your cooking will give it an earthy flavor and works particularly well in sauce, syrup, and marinade
- The most expensive coffee in the world is Black Ivory It's produced from the partially-digested coffee cherries eaten and pooped out by Thai elephants!

From chili to cupcakes, and polenta to pudding and pasta, cooking and baking with coffee is a great way to perk up sweet and savory recipes.

Breakfast and Brunch

Cappuccino French Toast with Coffee Cream

When the weekend comes around, spoil your family with this gourmet-style French toast topped with indulgent coffee cream.

Servings: 4

Total Time: 40mins

Ingredients:

- 2 tbsp coffee powder
- 2 tbsp sugar
- 1 cup almond milk
- 4 eggs
- 8 thickly-cut bread slices (halved to yield 16 half-slices, divided)
- ⅓ cup dark or milk chocolate chips (divided)
- Butter (to grease)
- Coffee Cream:
- ½ cup reduced-fat thickened whipping cream
- ½ tsp coffee powder
- 1 tbsp powdered sugar
- Cocoa powder (to dust, optional)

Directions:

First, prepare the French toast. In a jug, whisk the coffee, sugar, and almond milk.

Add the eggs, and whisk to combine.

Transfer the mixture to a 9x13" shallow dish.

Place 8 half-slices of bread on top of the egg mixture.

Scatter half of the chocolate chips over the top of the bread, and top with the remaining half-slices of bread to create sandwiches. Soak the sandwiches in the egg mixture for 5 minutes. Flip the bread over and soak for another 5 minutes.

Preheat a lightly buttered skillet or griddle,

When hot, in batches, cook the sandwiches until browned on both sides, cooked through, and the chocolate chips melted.

In the meantime, prepare the coffee cream. In a bowl, at moderate to high speed, beat the cream, coffee, and powdered sugar, until the mixture starts to thicken. Continue to beat to create whipped cream.

To serve, spoon the coffee cream over the French toast, sprinkle with cocoa and serve.

Cook's Note: If serving as a dessert or sweet treat rather than at breakfast or brunch, consider serving with a dollop of coffee flavor ice cream!

Cheddar Polenta with Sausage and Red Eye Gravy

The coffee-infused gravy is the star of the show for this savory brunch recipe to share.

Servings: 4

Total Time: N/A*

Ingredients:

Polenta:

- 2 tbsp olive oil
- 3 cups water
- 1 tsp salt
- 1 cup polenta
- ½ cup scallion (minced)
- ½ cup Cheddar cheese (grated)
- Oil (as needed, for brushing)

Sausages and gravy:

- 4 tbsp butter (butter)
- 4 breakfast-style sage breakfast sausage patties
- 2 tbsp flour
- 1 tsp sugar
- 1 cup brewed black coffee (cooled)

Directions:

For the polenta, which you can make the night before it is needed.

In a pan, heat the olive oil. Add the water and salt and bring to a boil.

Stream in the polenta while continually stirring, and bring to a boil. Turn the heat down while stirring, and simmer for approximately 12 minutes, or until creamy. Toss in the scallions and grated Cheddar.

Using parchment paper, line a sheet pan. Brush oil all over the sheet pan.

Spread the polenta out over the pan to a thickness of around ¾". Allow the polenta to cool and cut out your preferred shapes using a cookie cutter.

To assemble the breakfast: In a large frying pan, melt 2 tablespoons of butter.

Sauté the polenta shapes until crisp on both sides.

Transfer 2 polenta shapes to each plate and keep warm in the oven.

In the same frying pan, cook the sausage patties until cooked through and browned all over.

Using a spatula, place 1 sausage on top of the polenta on each plate and return to the oven.

With the remaining butter and flour, make a roux. Toast until nutty brown, and stir in the sugar. Allow the mixture to caramelize before adding the brewed coffee. You will need to scrape up all the bits from the bottom of the pan while boiling until the mixture thickens. Season with salt and pepper, and add a splash of boiling water if needed to achieve a thinner consistency.

Remove the plates from the oven.

Pour the gravy over the sausage patties and polenta, and serve.

*Total time will depend on whether or not you prepare the polenta in advance

Chili Mocha Cupcakes

Espresso powder adds a rich flavor to the frosting of these moist and spicy cupcakes, which are perfect for serving at your next brunch get-together.

Servings: 6-12*

Total Time: 1hr

Ingredients:

Cupcakes:

- 1 cup all-purpose flour
- 1 cup granulated sugar
- ½ cup cocoa powder
- 1 tsp baking powder
- ½ tsp bicarbonate of soda
- ½ tsp salt
- 2 tbsp espresso powder
- 1 tsp cinnamon
- ½ tsp cayenne pepper
- ¼ tsp smoked paprika
- ½ cup milk
- ¼ cup vegetable oil
- 1 large egg
- ½ tsp vanilla extract
- ½ cup water (boiling)

Frosting:

- 1 cup unsalted butter (room temperature)
- 2½ cups confectioner's sugar
- 1½ tsp vanilla extract
- 1 tbsp espresso powder
- Cayenne pepper (for dusting)

Directions:

Preheat the main oven to 325 degrees F. Using cupcake liners, line a muffin pan.

In a bowl, whisk flour, sugar, cocoa powder, baking powder, bicarbonate of soda, salt, espresso, cinnamon, cayenne and smoked paprika.

To the flour mixture, add the milk, vegetable oil, egg, and vanilla extract. With a hand mixer or using the paddle attachment of an electric stand mixer, on moderate speed, mix until combine.

Stop mixing, and pour in the boiling water. At high speed, beat for 60 seconds to aerate the batter.

Evenly divide the batter between the muffin cups.

Bake in the preheated oven for around 18 minutes, until springy to the touch.

Remove the cupcakes from the oven and set them aside to cool before frosting.

To prepare the frosting: In a bowl, beat the butter until fluffy and light. Add the confectioner's sugar, vanilla extract, and espresso powder, and beat until fluffy and incorporated.

When the cupcakes are completely cool, frost and dust with cayenne pepper.

*Number of servings will depend on the size of the muffin pan

Chocolate Coffee-Kick Granola

Healthy rolled oats combine with chia seeds, cocoa powder, and espresso powder to create the perfect breakfast granola to wake up even the sleepiest caffeine-lover.

Servings: 6

Total Time: 30mins

Ingredients:

- 3 cups old fashioned rolled oats
- 1 tsp vanilla extract
- ½ cup turbinado sugar
- ¼ cup chia seeds
- 1 tbsp espresso powder
- ⅓ cup unsweetened cocoa powder
- ½ cup coconut oil (melted)
- ½ cup semisweet chocolate chips (divided)

Directions:

Preheat the main oven to 300 degrees F.

In a bowl, combine oats, vanilla extract, sugar, chia seeds, espresso powder, cocoa powder, and mix well to combine.

Add the melted coconut oil, and mix well.

In a single layer, add the mixture to a large cookie sheet. Bake, undisturbed, in the oven for 20 minutes.

After 20 minutes, remove from the oven, add half of the chocolate chips and mix gently to combine. Increase the oven temperature to 325-350 degrees F, and bake for another 2-4 minutes to melt the chocolate.

Remove the cookie sheet from the oven, scatter over the remaining chocolate chips and allow to cool in the pan. Set aside for 10 minutes.

Enjoy as a yogurt topping or as a pop-in-the-mouth snack.

Store the granola in a resealable jar at room temperature for up to 7 days.

Coffee Buttermilk Pancakes

How do you like your pancakes in the morning? We like ours flavored with black coffee and served with sweet maple syrup!

Servings: 8-10

Total Time: 40mins

Ingredients:

- 2 cups all-purpose flour
- ¼ cup granulated sugar
- 1 tsp bicarbonate of soda
- ½ tsp salt
- 2 eggs
- 1½ cups brewed black coffee
- 2 cups buttermilk
- 3 tbsp unsalted butter
- 5 tsp canola oil (divided)
- Maple syrup (to serve, optional)
- Confectioner's sugar (to dust, optional)
- Butter (to serve, optional)

Directions:

Preheat the main oven to 200 degrees F.

In a bowl, whisk the flour with granulated sugar, bicarbonate of soda, and salt.

Melt the butter.

In a second bowl, whisk eggs with cool brewed coffee, buttermilk, and melted butter.

Add the dry to the wet ingredients, and stir. There may be some lumps remaining in the batter.

Over moderate to low heat, heat a pan. Add 1 teaspoon canola oil to the pan and heat.

Pour ½ cup batter into the pan, and cook on each side for 3 minutes. Repeat the process with the remaining batter, adding more oil to the pan as needed.

Keep the pancakes warm in the oven.

Serve the pancakes with maple syrup, dust with confectioner's sugar, and top with a knob of butter,

Coffee Glazed Brown Sugar Bacon

The tempting waft of coffee and bacon is more than enough to raise those sleepy heads from their beds.

Servings: 8

Total Time: 40mins

Ingredients:

- 1 pound thick-cut bacon slices
- 1 tbsp ground coffee

Glaze:

- ½ cup packed brown sugar
- 2 tbsp coffee (freshly brewed)

Directions:

Preheat the main oven to 375 degrees F. Using parchment paper, line a roasting pan. Place a flat baking rack on top of the pan.

Lay the bacon slices, overlapping slightly on the rack.

Scatter ground coffee over the bacon.

In a bowl, for the glaze, combine the brown sugar with the brewed coffee, stirring to blend and create a paste-like consistency.

Brush the bacon with half of the brown sugar mixture.

Bake the bacon in the oven for 15 minutes. Flip the slices over, and brush with the remaining brown sugar glaze. Continue to bake for an additional 10 minutes.

Remove from the oven and serve.

Coffee Nut Loaf

This moist coffee nut loaf, warmly spiced with cinnamon, is perfect for breakfast or brunch.

Servings: 16

Total Time: 1hr 15mins

Ingredients:

- 2¼ cups all-purpose flour
- 2 tsp ground cinnamon
- 2 tsp baking powder
- ½ tsp salt
- 1 tbsp water (hot)
- 3 tbsp coffee granules
- ⅓ cup butter (softened)
- 1½ cups granulated sugar
- 1½ cups sour cream
- 2 large eggs
- 1 cup nuts (chopped and divided)

Directions:

Preheat the main oven to 350 degrees F. Grease a 9x5" loaf pan.

In a bowl, combine flour, cinnamon, baking powder, and salt.

In a small bowl, combine the hot water with the coffee granules, stirring to dissolve.

In another bowl, combine softened butter and sugar. Add sour cream and eggs, and beat until creamy.

A little at a time, beat in the flour mixture from Step 2, alternating with the coffee mixture.

Fold in ¾ cup of nuts.

Spread the batter evenly into the prepared loaf pan.

Scatter the remaining nuts over the batter.

Bake in the preheated oven for 1 hour 5 minutes to 1 hour 10 minutes, until springy to the touch.

Remove from the oven and cool while in the pan, on a wire rack for 15 minutes.

Remove from the pan, and allow to completely cool on a wire baking rack.

Slice, serve and share.

Coffee Oatmeal

If you can't function without a morning cup of coffee, why not kick things up a notch and start the day with a bowl of coffee oatmeal?

Servings: 1

Total Time: 7mins

Ingredients:

- ½ cup rolled oats
- ¾ cup milk
- ¼ cup coffee (brewed and cooled)
- A pinch of salt
- Honey (to sweeten, optional)
- 1 tsp vanilla extract

Directions:

In a pot over moderate heat, combine the rolled oats, milk, brewed coffee, and salt. Cook for around 5 minutes.

Taste and sweeten with honey.

Stir in the vanilla extract and cook until you achieve your preferred consistency.

Macchiato Muffins

If you are a fan of a particular American multinational chain of coffeehouses, you will love this copycat muffin recipe!

Servings: 12

Total Time: 1hr

Ingredients:

- 2 cups flour
- ½ tsp salt
- 1 tbsp baking powder
- ¾ cup vanilla sugar
- 1 cup milk
- 1 egg
- 2 tbsp coffee granules
- ½ cup butter (melted and cooled)
- 3½ ounces semisweet chocolate chips
- ¼ cup store-bought caramel sauce (optional, to serve)

Directions:

Preheat the main oven to 375 degrees F. Grease a 12-cup muffin pan.

In a mixing bowl, combine flour, baking powder, salt, and vanilla sugar.

In a small bowl, combine the milk, egg, and coffee granules, stirring to dissolve the coffee.

Add the melted butter and mix thoroughly to combine.

Pour the coffee into the flour-sugar mixture and stir until just combined.

Fold in the chocolate chips, taking care, not to overwork.

Evenly divide the batter between the 12 muffin cups.

Bake in the preheated oven for 15-20 minutes, until springy to the touch.

Remove from the oven and cool for 5 minutes, while in the pan, before placing on a wire baking rack, to cool completely.

Drizzle with salted caramel sauce and enjoy.

Red Eye Eggs Benedict

A classic Eggs Benedict breakfast dish gets a Kentucky makeover with a Red Eye-style Hollandaise sauce.

Servings: 4

Total Time: 35mins

Ingredients:

Red Eye Hollandaise:

- 8 egg yolks
- ½ tbsp water
- 1 pound butter (melted and clarified)
- Freshly squeezed juice from 2 lemons
- 1 tsp salt
- A couple of dashes of hot sauce

Eggs Benedict:

- 4 cups water
- ½ tsp white vinegar
- A pinch of salt
- 4 baking powder biscuits
- 8 ounces country ham (thinly sliced)
- 1 cup strong coffee (brewed)
- ½ tsp brown sugar
- 8 eggs

Directions:

For the sauce, set a stainless steel bowl carefully over a pan of simmering water. Beat the egg yolks and water until stiff peaks start to appear. Slowly add the melted and clarified butter, fresh lemon juice, salt, and hot sauce, until combine. Put the sauce to one side.

In a pan, for the eggs, heat water to a simmer. Add the white vinegar and a pinch of salt to the water, and maintain a simmer.

Heat the baking powder biscuits, and split.

In a frying pan, sauté the ham, and place on each biscuit half.

Deglaze the pan with coffee, add the sugar.

In the meantime, heat the sauce and poach the eggs in the simmering water.

To serve, add the coffee mixture to the sauce and season to taste.

Top the ham and biscuits with the poached eggs, spoon over the red-eye hollandaise and serve.

Top Tip: Timing is everything with this recipe

Lite Bites and Mains

Asian-Style Pork Ribs with Coffee BBQ Sauce

Are you looking for an alternative to your favorite honey BBQ ribs? Then it's time to get creative with coffee!

Servings: 4

Total Time: 1hr

Ingredients:

Marinade:

- ½ tsp salt
- 2 tbsp oyster sauce
- 1 tsp sesame oil
- 5 tbsp cornflour
- ½ tsp bicarbonate of soda
- 3 tbsp water
- 1 egg (lightly beaten)

Ribs:

- 1 pound pork spare rib
- Oil (for deep frying)
- 1 tsp sesame seeds (to serve)
- 1 spring onion (trimmed and finely chopped, to serve)
- A bunch of coriander (picked over, to serve)

Sauce/Glaze:

- 2 tbsp coffee granules
- 3 tbsp brown sugar
- 2 tbsp white sugar
- 2 garlic cloves (peeled and finely sliced)
- 3 tbsp BBQ sauce
- 1 tbsp rice wine vinegar
- 1 tbsp dark soy sauce

- 5 tbsp water
- 1 cinnamon stick
- 3 whole dried chilies

Directions:

In a bowl, combine the marinade ingredients (salt, oyster sauce, sesame oil, cornflour, bicarb, water, and beaten egg).

Add the ribs to the marinade, and transfer to the fridge for 30-60 minutes.

In a pan, heat the oil to 325 degrees F.

Remove the ribs from the marinade, shaking off any excess, and fry until a deep golden color, all over.

In a frying pan, combine the sauce ingredients (coffee granules, brown sugar, white sugar, garlic, BBQ sauce, rice wine vinegar, dark soy sauce, water, cinnamon stick, and whole dried chilies). Bring the mixture to a simmer and reduce until the sauce thickens and can coat the back of a spoon.

Add the pork ribs to the sauce, toss evenly, and well coat. Reduce the sauce more until it is the consistency of a sticky glaze.

When the ribs are ready to serve, remove and discard the cinnamon stick and dried chilies.

Garnish the ribs and sauce with sesame seed and a sprinkling of spring onions and chopped coriander.

Serve and enjoy.

Baked Cod with Coffee Butter

Switch up fish. And prepare fresh cod baked with coffee butter. It makes a welcome change from the usual parsley or cheese-based sauces.

Servings: 4

Total Time: 20mins

Ingredients:

- Nonstick baking spray
- 1½ pounds fresh cod (rinsed, patted dry, and de-boned)
- 3 tbsp salted butter
- 1 tbsp freshly squeezed lemon juice
- ⅜ tsp garlic powder
- ⅜ tsp freshly ground black pepper
- ⅜ - ½ tsp coffee extract (to taste)
- Salt (to season)

Directions:

Preheat your main oven to 400 degrees. Spritz a rimmed baking pan with nonstick baking spray.

Lay the de-boned cod on the baking pan.

In 20 second increments, in the microwave, melt the butter.

Add the fresh lemon juice, garlic powder, black pepper, and coffee extract to the butter. Whisk the butter mixture until the ingredients are combined.

Pour the coffee butter over the fish.

Bake the fish in the oven for 15 minutes until it flakes easily when using a fork.

Season the fish with salt to taste.

Serve and enjoy.

Beef Chili with Coffee

Coffee is, without doubt, the secret ingredient to successful beef chili. It adds an earthy and rich flavor to the meat and combines well with cumin and cayenne to create a tasty main for older members of the family to enjoy.

Servings: 8

Total Time: 2hrs 20mins

Ingredients:

- 2 tbsp oil
- 2 pounds ground beef
- 2 cups onions (peeled and chopped)
- ½ cup green bell pepper (chopped)
- 3 garlic cloves (peeled and crushed)
- 1 tsp chili powder
- 1 tsp cumin
- 1 (15½ ounces) can chopped tomatoes
- 2 cups strong coffee (brewed)
- 1 cup cold water
- 1 (4 ounces) can chopped green chilies
- 1½ tsp salt
- ¼ tsp cayenne pepper

Directions:

Heat the oil in a pan over moderate heat.

Add the ground beef, onions, bell pepper, and garlic, and cook until the meat is browned all over.

Stir in the chili powder and cumin.

Next, add the canned tomatoes, brewed coffee, water, green chilies, salt, and cayenne pepper.

Cover the pan with a lid, and cook for 60 minutes. Remove the pan's lid and continue to cook for another 60 minutes.

Serve and enjoy.

Beef Fillet with Café Au Lait Sauce

Next time you host a dinner party, get fancy with this fillet steak; forget black peppercorn sauce, and instead opt for this creamy coffee-mushroom sauce.

Servings: 6

Total Time: 3hrs 40mins

Ingredients:

Sauce:

- 2 cups cream
- 1¾ ounces coffee beans
- 5¼ ounces crimini mushrooms (halved)
- 1 tbsp butter
- ½ cup beef stock
- Sea salt and black pepper (to season)

Fillet:

- 1 tsp olive oil
- 4 pounds whole beef fillet
- 1 ounce butter (chopped)
- 1 tsp fresh thyme

Directions:

For the sauce: In a pan, bring the cream and coffee beans to a boil. Remove the pan from the heat and allow the coffee to infuse the cream while occasionally stirring for 3 hours.

Preheat the main oven to 390 degrees F. Over high heat, heat a large pan until it is smoking hot.

Add oil to the pan, and sear the beef fillet until browned on both sides. Remove from the pan, and transfer to a baking tray.

Dot the meat with a few blobs of butter, and scatter over the thyme. Roast the meat in the oven for 15-20 minutes or until cooked to your preferred level of doneness. Set aside to rest for 10 minutes before slicing.

Continue with the sauce in a frying pan over very high heat, frying the mushrooms in butter until golden brown. Remove the mushrooms from the pan.

Strain the coffee cream mixture into the pan, and bring to a boil. Return the browned mushrooms to the pan and pour in the stock. Reduce the sauce for 3 minutes and pour over the beef fillet, and serve.

Chicken Coffee Curry

It is incredible how coffee, a pantry staple, can elevate so many favorite recipes. In this curry recipe, it adds depth of flavor and a pleasing aroma. The bitterness of the black coffee is perfectly counter-balanced by the sweet honey and Asian spices.

Servings: 2

Total Time: 1hr 20mins

Ingredients:

- A splash of olive oil
- 2 chicken breasts
- 2-3 whole garlic cloves (peeled)
- 1 cup onions (peeled and sliced)
- 1 cup green peas
- 1 tbsp smooth peanut butter
- 1 tsp curry powder
- ¼ tsp cardamom
- 2 tbsp honey
- 1 cup soy milk
- 1 cup strong black coffee (brewed)
- 2 portions Basmati rice (to serve, optional)

Directions:

Add a splash of oil to a pan and set over moderate heat.

Add the chicken breasts to the pan together with the cloves of garlic and sliced onions. Fry the chicken until golden.

Add the peas, peanut butter, curry powder, cardamom, honey, and milk to the pan. Stir to combine and cover with a lid to allow the flavors to infuse. Simmer over low heat for 60 minutes, while occasionally stirring, to prevent the mixture from burning.

Remove the pan's lid, and add the coffee, stirring to combine thoroughly. Cook the curry until thickened.

Serve with rice and enjoy.

Coffee-Brined Chicken Drumsticks

Next time you are making chicken drumsticks for grown-ups, make sure they are super-juicy by preparing them in a sweet and spicy coffee brine

Servings: 4

Total Time: 2hrs 40mins

Ingredients:

- 2 cups water
- 1½ cups strongly brewed coffee
- ¼ salt
- 3 tbsp sugar
- 2 tbsp chili powder
- ½ tsp crushed red pepper
- 3 garlic cloves (peeled and crushed)
- 1 cinnamon stick
- 2½ pounds chicken drumsticks

Directions:

In a bowl, stir the water with coffee, salt, and sugar until the sugar and salt are entirely dissolved. Next, stir in the chili powder, crushed red pepper, garlic, and cinnamon stick.

Add the chicken drumsticks to the bowl, and top with a small plate to ensure the chicken is submerged.

Cover and transfer to the fridge for 2-4 hours.

Preheat the broiler.

Remove the chicken wings from the brine, discard the brine, and transfer to a broiler pan.

Approximately 4-6" away from the heat, broil the chicken drumsticks until browned for approximately 10 minutes. Then, flip the drumsticks over and broil for another 10 minutes, or until browned.

Preheat the main oven to 350 degrees F.

Transfer the broiler pan to the center rack of the oven, and bake until the drumsticks are no longer pink, for an additional 10-15 minutes.

Serve, and enjoy.

Coffee Coconut Shrimp

Once you have tasted these sweet and crisp coffee coconut shrimp, there is no going back!

Servings: 2

Total Time: 18mins

Ingredients:

- 1 ½ cups flour
- ½ tsp salt
- ¾ cup whole milk
- ¼ cup strong coffee
- 2 tbsp coconut milk
- ½ cup sweet shredded coconut
- 1 cup panko breadcrumbs
- 12 large fresh shrimp (peeled, deveined, tails-on)
- 6-8 tbsp coconut oil

Directions:

In a bowl, combine flour, salt, whole milk, coffee, and coconut milk, until smooth.

In a second bowl, combine the shredded coconut with the breadcrumbs.

Dip the shrimp first in the flour-milk mixture and then into the coconut breadcrumb mixture. Make sure each shrimp is evenly and well coated.

Over moderately high heat, heat the coconut oil. When hot, in a single layer, and in batches if necessary, add the coated shrimp to the pan. Cook the shrimp for around 2 minutes on each side until crisp, browned and cooked through. Transfer to a paper towel-lined plate until ready to serve.

Coffee Crusted Lamb

Who doesn't like a tender and juicy leg of lamb? But here, served with a coffee crust, it is a real game-changer.

Servings: 6-8

Total Time: 9hrs 35mins

Ingredients:

- 1 tbsp freshly ground coffee
- ½ cup boiling water
- 1 onion (peeled and coarsely chopped)
- 3 garlic cloves (peeled and crushed)
- 1 tbsp fresh rosemary (coarsely chopped)
- 1 tbsp fresh parsley (coarsely chopped)
- 1 tbsp fresh thyme (coarsely chopped)
- 1 tbsp honey
- 1 tsp cracked black pepper
- Pink Himalayan salt (to season)
- 1 (2½ pounds) boneless leg of lamb

Directions:

Add the coffee to a heatproof bowl. Pour the boiling water over the coffee, and brew for 3-5 minutes before combining in a processor with onion, garlic, rosemary, parsley, thyme, honey, and black pepper until smooth. Season the mixture liberally with Himalayan salt.

Place the lamb in a large dish, and coat all over with the coffee mixture. Cover the dish and transfer overnight to the fridge to marinate.

Preheat the main oven to 390 degrees F.

Place the leg of lamb on a wire rack, set inside a roasting pan.

Add ¾" of water to the pan, and roast for 40 minutes. Turn the heat down to 320 degrees F and continue to roast for an additional 40 minutes, or until the lamb is cooked to your preferred level of doneness. Cover, and allow to rest for 10 minutes before serving.

Coffee Marinated Sirloin Steak

This coffee marinated sirloin steak is better than any you will find in fancy restaurants.

Servings: 6

Total Time: 8hrs 35mins

Ingredients:

- 6 tbsp butter
- 2 tbsp sesame seeds
- 1 medium onion (peeled and chopped)
- 4 garlic cloves (peeled and chopped)
- 1 cup strong black coffee (brewed)
- 1 cup soy sauce
- 2 tbsp white vinegar
- 2 tbsp Worcestershire sauce
- 2 pounds (1" thick) beef top sirloin steak

Directions:

In a small frying pan, in butter, toast the sesame seeds.

To the pan, add the onion and garlic, and sauté until tender.

Combine the coffee, soy sauce, white vinegar, Worcestershire sauce, and toasted sesame seed mixture in a bowl.

Pour half of the mixture into a shallow dish.

Add the steak to the dish, and turn to evenly and well coat.

Cover with a lid and transfer to the fridge overnight while occasionally turning. Cover and transfer the remaining marinade to the fridge, also.

The following day, drain and discard the marinade from the meat.

Over moderate to high heat, grill the steak for 6-10 minutes on each side or until it is cooked to your preferred level of doneness.

Warm the reserved marinade and serve alongside the steak.

Coffee Red Lentil Soup

Coffee-lovers everywhere rejoice. This coffee red lentil soup is worth coming home for!

Servings: 6

Total Time: 30mins

Ingredients:

- 3 tbsp olive oil
- 1 onion (peeled and minced)
- 1 carrot (trimmed and diced)
- 1 celery stalk (trimmed and diced)
- 8 ounces mushrooms (sliced)
- 4 garlic cloves (peeled and minced)
- 2 tsp powdered turmeric
- 2 tbsp ginger (peeled and freshly grated)
- 1 tsp ground cumin
- 1 tsp ground coriander
- 1 cup red lentils (rinsed in cold water)
- ½ cup basmati rice (rinsed in cold water)
- 8 cups chicken or vegetable broth
- 2 tsp ground coffee
- Salt and freshly ground pepper (to season)
- 1 (19 ounces) can chickpeas (drained and rinsed)
- Freshly squeezed lime juice (to garnish)
- Fresh cilantro (chopped, to garnish)

Directions:

In a large pot, over moderate heat, heat the oil. Add the onion, carrot, celery, and mushrooms to the pan, and cook for 5-10 minutes while stirring frequently.

Add the garlic, turmeric, ginger, cumin, and coriander, and over moderate to low heat, cook for 3 minutes.

Next, add the lentils, basmati rice, broth, and ground coffee. Bring the mixture to a boil.

Season with salt and black pepper to taste and simmer until the lentils are tender, for around 20 minutes.

Stir in the chickpeas and heat through.

Before serving the soup, add a squeeze of fresh lime juice and garnish with cilantro.

Coffee-Rubbed Salmon with Orange Salsa

This salmon main is perfect served with brown rice or baby new potatoes and salad.

Servings: 6

Total Time: 40mins

Ingredients:

Rub:

- 2 tbsp light brown sugar
- 2 tsp ground coffee
- 2 tsp ground coriander
- 1 tsp smoked paprika
- ¾ tsp kosher salt
- ½ tsp cayenne pepper

Salmon:

- 1½ pounds salmon fillet (cut into 6 even portions)
- 1 small shallot (thinly sliced)
- 2 tbsp sherry vinegar
- ¼ tsp salt
- 6 portions brown rice (cooked, to serve, optional)

Salsa:

- 2 large navel oranges
- 2 tbsp fresh parsley (chopped)
- 2 tbsp extra-virgin olive oil

Directions:

Place your oven rack in the lower third of your main oven, and preheat to 450 degrees F.

In a bowl, combine the brown sugar with coffee, coriander, paprika, ¾ teaspoon salt, and cayenne.

Lay the salmon portion on a baking sheet and rub it all over with the rub.

Roast the salmon on the rack in the preheated oven until cooked through, for 6-8 minutes, or until opaque in the center.

In the meantime, combine the shallot, vinegar, and remaining salt in a bowl. Allow to stand for 5 minutes.

Prepare the salsa. Zest the navel oranges, removing and discarding the peel, pith, and pips and coarsely chopping the fruit.

Stir the orange zest, fruit, parsley, and olive oil into the shallot mixture to combine.

Serve the salsa with the cooked salmon on a bed of brown rice and enjoy.

Coffee-Rubbed Pork Tenderloin with Espresso-Honey Glace

This smoky-sweet glace sauce is perfect for pork. Enjoy!

Servings: 4

Total Time: 1hr

Ingredients:

Coffee Spice Rub:

- 2 tbsp packed dark brown sugar
- 2 tbsp espresso powder
- 1 tbsp kosher salt
- 2 tsp honey powder
- 1 tsp garlic powder
- 1 tsp smoked paprika
- 1 tsp sweet paprika
- ¾ tsp freshly ground black pepper
- ½ tsp onion powder
- ½ tsp unsweetened cocoa powder
- ¼ tsp ground dried chipotle pepper

Pork:

- 1 (1½ pounds) pork tenderloin
- 2 tbsp olive oil (divided)

Glace Sauce:

- ½ cup water
- 4 tsp beef demi-glace
- 1 tbsp Dijon mustard
- 1 tsp honey powder

Directions:

Preheat the main oven to 400 degrees F.

In a bowl, combine brown sugar, espresso powder, salt, honey powder, garlic powder, sweet and smoked paprika, black pepper, onion powder, cocoa powder, and ground chipotle. Mix well and transfer 1 tablespoon of the rub into a bowl.

Place the pork on a clean worktop, remove the silver skin, and with kitchen paper towels, pat dry.

Scatter a large amount of the coffee spice rub all over the pork tenderloin with your fingers. Drizzle 1 tablespoon of oil over the pork and rub into the meat. Set aside to rest for 10 minutes at room temperature.

In a large oven-proof skillet over moderate to high heat, heat 1 tablespoon of oil.

Add the pork to the skillet and cook for approximately 8 minutes, until browned on all sides.

Transfer the skillet to the oven, and roast the pork until slightly pink in the middle for around 15 minutes. The meat is cooked when it registers an internal temperature of around 145 degrees F. Remove from the oven and allow to rest on a platter for around 10 minutes.

Next, prepare the glace. Over moderate heat and in the same skillet,

combine 1 tablespoon of the reserved coffee spice water, water, beef demi-glace, mustard, and honey powder. Cook, while frequently stirring for 3-4 minutes, or until the sauce thickens.

Slice the pork tenderloin into rounds and drizzle with the glace sauce.

Dark Roast Coffee-Infused Risotto

Top this delicious risotto with a fried egg for breakfast or brunch as a side or serve cold as a salad topper and enjoy as a lite bite to share.

Servings: N/A*

Total Time: 25mins

Ingredients:

- 2 cups beef stock
- 2 tbsp olive oil
- 1 shallot (finely chopped)
- ½ cup mushrooms (sliced)
- ½ tbsp dark roast coffee (finely ground)
- 1 cup Arborio rice
- Water (as needed)
- Salt and freshly ground black pepper (to season)
- Sour cream (to taste)

Directions:

In a small saucepan, over low heat, bring the stock to a boil.

In a large skillet, heat the oil and cook the shallots until softened over moderate heat.

Add the mushrooms to the shallots and cook for an additional 2 minutes.

Next, add the coffee and Arborio rice, and stir thoroughly to combine. Pour in the beef stock, and over high heat, bring to a boil.

Turn the heat down, and cook in 4-5 minutes increments, stirring until the rice is al dente. You may want to add a splash more water if needed.

Reduce to low heat, and season with salt and black pepper to taste. Stir well and serve hot, topped with a dollop of sour cream.

*Servings will depend on how you serve the risotto

French Onion and Coffee Soup

If you think you can't improve on French onion soup, think again! All you need to add for a little Oh là là is a cup or two of freshly brewed French roast coffee!

Servings: 8

Total Time: 2hrs

Ingredients:

- 2 tbsp olive oil
- 4 pounds red onions (peeled and chopped)
- 8 cups vegetable stock
- 1½ cups French roast coffee (brewed)
- 2 bay leaves
- 1 tsp mochi mugi or barley
- 1 garlic clove (peeled and smashed)
- A small sprig of fresh thyme
- A small sprig of fresh marjoram
- Salt (to season)
- 1 French baguette
- 2 cups Gruyere cheese (grated)

Directions:

In a Dutch oven, in a pan over moderate to low heat, warm olive oil. To the pan, add the onions, tossing to coat. Turn the heat up to moderately high and while stirring every 10 minutes until they start to caramelize. You may need to reduce the heat to prevent them from burning. They are ready when they are a jam-like consistency and a deep golden brown color. This step could take as long as 50-60 minutes.

Pour in the stock and coffee and add the bay leaves, barley, garlic, thyme, marjoram and bring to a low simmer. Cook the soup for 30 minutes.

Preheat the main oven to 350 degrees F.

Meanwhile, prepare the croûtes. First, slice the baguette into 1" thick slices.

Arrange the slices of bread on a baking sheet lined with parchment paper. Brush the bread with oil and bake them in the oven for around 15 minutes, until toasted.

When the soup is ready, season with salt to taste.

Ladle the soup into ramekins, top with 2 croûtes, and garnish with Gruyere cheese.

Place the ramekins under a hot grill and broil until the cheese is bubbling and melted.

Serve and enjoy.

Italian Cheese, Breaded Chicken with Coffee Penne

The subtle bitterness of the black coffee is counter-balanced by the flavor of three varieties of Italian cheese and sweet onions to create an upscale pasta dish for two to share.

Servings: 2

Total Time: 1hr 30mins

Ingredients:

Chicken:

- 2 boneless, skinless chicken breasts
- 2 cups flour
- 3 eggs
- 1½ cups breadcrumbs
- 2 tbsp dried parsley
- ¾ cup Pecorino Romano (grated)
- ¾ cup Parmesan cheese (freshly grated)
- Salt and freshly ground black pepper
- Olive oil (as needed)

Penne:

- 2 tbsp butter
- 1 onion (peeled and sliced)
- 1 poblano pepper (sliced)
- 3 garlic cloves (peeled and minced)
- 1 cup strong black coffee (brewed)
- 16 ounces mini penne pasta
- ½ cup ricotta cheese
- 1 cup Parmesan cheese (freshly grated)
- ¼ cup whole milk
- ¼ cup parsley (chopped)

Directions:

First, slice each chicken breast horizontally in half to create thinner breasts.

Place the chicken one piece at a time on a chopping board on top of a sheet of kitchen wrap. Top the chicken with another sheet of wrap. Pound the chicken to make it thinner and an even thickness. Repeat until each portion is prepared.

Add the flour to a shallow bowl, the egg to a second shallow bowl,

Combine the breadcrumbs, parsley, grated pecorino, and Parmesan and add the mixture to a third shallow bowl.

Season all three bowls with salt and freshly ground black pepper.

Remove the wrap from the chicken portions, bread each first in the flour, then the egg, and finally the breadcrumb mix. You will need to shake off any excess as you go and lightly press the breading firmly but gently onto the chicken. Repeat with one more additional coating of egg and then breadcrumb mix in this order (flour, egg, breadcrumb mix, egg, and breadcrumb mix).

Add olive oil to a pan to a depth of around ½".

Fry the chicken in the pan until crispy and browned on both sides.

Preheat the main oven to 200 degrees F.

Transfer the fried chicken to a baking sheet and place it in the oven to keep warm while you prepare the penne.

For the penne: Bring a deep pan of water to a boil.

Add the butter to a pan over moderate heat. Add the onions to the pan, season with salt, and cook for around 30 minutes, until browned.

Next, add the poblano pepper and cook for an additional 5 minutes. Next, add the garlic and cook for 60 seconds. Finally, pour in the brewed coffee.

Cook the pasta in a pan of boiling water, according to the package direction, and until al dente.

While the pasta is cooking, allow the coffee mixture to simmer.

When the penne is al dente, strain the pasta cooking liquid directly into the sauce.

Remove the pan from the heat, stir in the ricotta and Parmesan cheeses, and stir thoroughly to coat. You may want to add a splash of milk to create a creamy consistency.

Remove the breaded chicken from the oven and slice.

Transfer the pasta to a serving bowl, and top with the sliced chicken.

Garnish with parsley and enjoy.

Mexican Turkey Mole with Espresso Coffee

Coffee is a popular ingredient in lots of Mexican dishes, and here in a rich tomato-based sauce, it transforms a good mole sauce into a great one!

Servings: 2

Total Time: 2hrs 30mins

Ingredients:

- 1 chipotle chili
- ½ tsp chili flakes
- 1 tsp sherry vinegar
- 1 tsp tomato paste
- 1 tbsp vegetable oil
- Oil (to cook, as needed)
- 1 pound 2 ounces turkey (chopped)
- ½ –1 tsp salt (to season)
- 1 onion (peeled and chopped)
- 1 garlic clove (peeled and crushed)
- 1 tsp ground cumin
- ½ tsp ground cinnamon
- 1 tbsp raspberry jam
- 1 tbsp ground almonds
- 7 ounces canned chopped tomatoes
- 2 shots espresso coffee
- ½ ounce dark chocolate (grated)
- White rice (steamed, to serve, optional)
- Sour cream (to serve, optional)
- Fresh parsley (chopped, to serve, optional)
- Lime wedges (to garnish)

Directions:

First, soak the chipotle chili in hot water for 20 minutes. Set the soaking water aside, remove and discard the stems and seeds from the chili and chop finely. Set the chopped chili to one side.

In a small bowl, combine the chili flakes, sherry vinegar, tomato paste, and vegetable oil. Put aside until needed.

Heat 1 tablespoon of oil in a pan.

Season the turkey with salt. Over high heat, brown the meat all over. Remove from the skillet and set aside.

Turn the heat down to moderate, and in the same skillet, cook the onion and garlic until softened for 5 minutes.

To the skillet, add the cumin and ground cinnamon and cook for another 2-3 minutes, until fragrant.

Stir in the jam and almonds, mixing thoroughly. Cook the mixture for 2-3 minutes.

Next, add the tomatoes, chipotle, chili paste from Step 2, and coffee. Finally, add 4-5 tablespoons of the chipotle soaking water put aside earlier. Season the mixture with salt and return the turkey to the pan. Cover with a lid and cook while occasionally stirring for 30 minutes.

Add the grated dark chocolate, and while covered, continue to cook for 20-25 minutes. You may need to add a splash of water to prevent the mixture from drying out.

Serve the mole on a bed of rice with a dollop of sour cream. Garnish with parsley and a lime wedge for squeezing.

Rigatoni with Coffee Spiced Pork and Beef Sausage

It is a good idea to make this pasta main one day ahead to allow the flavors to infuse; we guarantee you won't be disappointed.

Servings: 6-8

Total Time: 25mins

Ingredients:

Sausage:

- 8 ounces ground pork
- 8 ounces ground beef
- 3½ tbsp coffee rub (of choice, any brand)

Pasta:

- 1 pound rigatoni pasta
- 1 yellow bell pepper (sliced into strips)
- 2 garlic cloves (peeled and minced)
- ½ cup dry white wine
- ¼ cup Irish stout
- ¾ cup heavy cream
- 10 cherry tomatoes (halved)
- 4 scallions (sliced on the bias)
- A large pinch of crushed red pepper flakes
- Salt and freshly ground pepper (to season)

Directions:

To prepare the sausage, in a bowl, combine the ground pork, ground beef, and coffee rub. Cover the bowl and transfer to the fridge for a minimum of 30 minutes and a maximum of 8 hours.

When you are ready to begin cooking, cook the pasta according to the package instructions and until al dente. Drain the pasta, and put to one side.

In the meantime, in a skillet over moderately high heat, brown the sausage mixture for 4-6 minutes.

Next, stir in the bell pepper and garlic.

Pour in the white wine and stout and simmer for 4-5 minutes, or until reduced by approximately 50 percent.

Fold in the cream and simmer for 2-3 minutes.

Finally, add the drained pasta, tomatoes, and scallions, stir gently to combine.

Season to taste with red pepper flakes, salt, and black pepper, and enjoy.

Roasted Espresso Coffee Chipotle Shrimp

If you are looking to impress your dinner guests but are short on time, these juicy shrimp will save the day.

Servings: 6

Total Time: 20mins

Ingredients:

- 2 pounds shrimp
- 2 tbsp brown sugar
- 1 tbsp dark roast finely ground coffee
- 1 tsp chipotle powder
- 3 mandarin oranges (sliced)
- 2-3 tbsp extra-virgin olive oil
- ½ tsp sea salt
- ½ tsp freshly ground black pepper

Directions:

Preheat the main oven to 400 degrees F. In a bowl, toss the shrimp with brown sugar, finely ground coffee, chipotle powder, slices of mandarin oranges, and 2 tablespoons of oil. Season the shrimp with salt and black pepper. Add the remaining oil to the shrimp if needed.

In a single layer, arrange the seasoned shrimp on a lightly greased sheet pan. Make sure that the mandarin orange slices are evenly spaced.

Roast the shrimp in the oven for 8-10 minutes, until firm, just pink, and cooked through.

Serve and enjoy.

Spicy Coffee-Baked Sweet Potatoes

These coffee-baked sweet potatoes are a sensory overload. They are colorful and flavorful and emit a subtle aroma of earthy spices, with a faint hint of freshly brewed coffee.

Servings: 2

Total Time: 1hr 20mins

Ingredients:

- 1 pound coffee beans
- 2 sweet potatoes (same size)

Spice Mixture:

- ½ tsp sea salt
- ½ tsp smoked paprika
- ⅛ tsp ground cinnamon
- A pinch of cayenne pepper
- A pinch of brown sugar
- 4 tbsp crème fraiche
- Zest of 1 fresh lime
- ½ cup fresh cilantro leaves

Directions:

Preheat the main oven to 375 degrees F.

Scatter the coffee beans evenly onto a baking sheet.

Using a metal fork, prick the sweet potatoes all over.

Nestle, the sweet potatoes into the coffee beans.

Transfer the baking sheet to the preheated oven and roast for 30 minutes. You will need to check on the beans every once in a while to ensure they aren't smoking. Smoking occurs when the oven is too hot, and if this happens, you will smell a burnt potato aroma.

When 30 minutes have elapsed, flip the potatoes over, and give the coffee beans a gentle stir.

Reduce the oven temperature to 350 degrees F, and continue to bake the potatoes until tender and their skins are collapsing. This step will take an additional 30-45 minutes more. The sweet potatoes are ready when you can pierce all the way through their skin and flesh using a blunt knife. Set aside until sufficiently cool enough to handle. When the coffee beans are cooled, discard.

For the spice mixture. In a bowl, combine the salt with smoked paprika, cinnamon, cayenne, and brown sugar.

Slice each sweet potato in half lengthwise and with a metal fork, fluff up the flesh.

Scatter the spice mixture evenly over each of the 4 sweet potato halves.

Garnish each one with 1 tablespoon crème fraiche, lime zest, and cilantro leaves.

Serve and enjoy.

Sweet Potato, Kale, and Ham Hash with Maple Syrup Red-Eye Gravy

Lots of flavor to this sweet potato, kale, and ham hash. Serve it with maple syrup and coffee infused gravy and transform a good meal into a great one!

Servings: 4

Total Time: 45mins

Ingredients:

- 10 ounces country-style ham (cut into bite-size pieces)
- 1 tbsp butter
- 1 leek, white parts only (chopped)
- 2 medium sweet potatoes (peeled and cut into ½" cubes)
- 1 cup black coffee (divided)
- ¼ cup pure maple syrup
- 3 cups kale (chopped)
- 2 garlic cloves (peeled and minced)
- 4-6 eggs
- A pinch of freshly ground black pepper (to season)

Directions:

Over moderately high heat, heat a large frying pan or skillet.

To the pan, add the ham and brown on both sides while occasionally stirring. Remove the ham from the pan and transfer to a bowl.

Without removing any ham fat, add the butter to the skillet. Next, add the leek, stirring until evenly and well coated in the fat and butter.

Next, add the sweet potato cubes, stirring to coat with the butter mixture. Cook the potatoes for 7 minutes while occasionally stirring.

Pour in ½ cup of black coffee and allow to simmer for an additional 7 minutes, until the potatoes are almost cooked but still retain a little crunch.

While the sweet potatoes are cooking, in a small bowl, combine the remaining coffee with maple syrup, and put to one side.

Add the kale and minced garlic to the skillet, and cook for around 4 minutes until the kale has just wilted.

Next, add the ham to the skillet.

Pour the coffee-maple syrup mixture over the top, stirring well to coat.

Create 4-6 wells in the ham hash. Break an egg into each well. Cover the pan with a lid and cook until the eggs are prepared to your preferred level of doneness.

Season with black pepper, and serve.

Sweet Treats & Desserts

Boozy Irish Cream Frosted Coffee Cupcakes

Cupcakes aren't just for kids, and these boozy coffee cupcakes are a sweet treat for over-21's only!

Servings: 18-20

Total Time: 1hr

Ingredients:

Cupcakes:

- 1 cup unsalted butter (room temperature)
- 2 cups sugar
- 4 eggs
- 1½ cups self-raising flour
- 1¼ cups all-purpose flour
- 1 cup strong brewed coffee
- ½ cup whole milk
- 1 tsp vanilla extract
- 1 rounded tsp espresso powder
- 1-3 tbsp Irish whiskey (to taste)

Frosting:

- 1 cup unsalted butter (room temperature)
- ¼ tsp salt
- 1 pound confectioner's sugar
- ½ cup Irish cream liqueur

Directions:

For the cupcakes: Preheat the main oven to 350 degrees F.

In the bowl of an electric mixer, cream the butter with the sugar until fluffy and light.

One at a time, add the eggs, beating well between additions until incorporated.

In a bowl, using a whisk, combine the self-raising and all-purpose flour.

Combine the coffee, milk, and vanilla extract and alternate adding the flour and coffee mixtures. You will need to start with the flour and end with the flour. Mix until just combined before adding the espresso powder.

Transfer the batter into an (18-20 cup) muffin pan lined with paper and bake in the oven for 15-20 minutes or until springy to the touch. Remove the cupcakes to a wire cooling rack and drizzle over your preferred amount of Irish whiskey. Allow to completely cool before frosting.

For the frosting: In the bowl of an electric mixer, beat the butter and salt until creamy. Then, a little at a time, add the confectioner's sugar, alternating with the Irish cream liqueur. Beat the mixture for 2-3 minutes, until creamy smooth.

Spread the frosting over the cupcakes and serve.

Cappuccino Muffins

When it's time for an afternoon break, why not spoil yourself with a double hit of coffee. Serve these delicious cappuccino muffins topped with espresso cream cheese along with a steaming mug of your favorite coffee blend.

Servings: 12-14

Total Time: 35mins

Ingredients:

Espresso Cream Cheese Topping:

- 4 ounces cream cheese (cubed)
- 1 tbsp sugar
- ½ tsp coffee granules
- ½ tsp vanilla extract
- ¼ cup mini semisweet chocolate chips

Muffins:

- 2 cups all-purpose flour
- ¾ cup sugar
- 1 tsp ground cinnamon
- 2½ tsp baking powder
- ½ tsp salt
- ½ cup butter (melted)
- 1 large egg
- 1 tsp vanilla extract
- ¾ cup mini semisweet chocolate chips

Directions:

In a food processor for the espresso spread, combine the cream cheese, sugar, coffee granules, vanilla extract, and mini semisweet chocolate chips. When blended, transfer to a bowl, cover, and place in the fridge until ready to serve.

For the muffins: In a large mixing bowl, combine the flour, sugar, baking powder, cinnamon, and salt.

Next, combine the melted butter, egg and vanilla extract. Finally, stir into the flour ingredients until just moistened.

Fold in the semisweet chocolate chips.

Line a 12-15 cup muffin pan with paper liners, and fill with the muffin mixture to around ⅔

Bake the muffins in the oven for 18-20 minutes, until springy to the touch.

Remove from the oven and cool for 5 minutes before removing the muffins from the pan and cooling on wire baking racks.

When the muffins are cooled, spread with the espresso cream cheese and serve slightly warm.

Choco-Coffee Covered Strawberries

These chocolate and coffee-covered strawberries are pop-in-the-mouth perfection.

Servings: 20

Total Time: 40mins

Ingredients:

- 1 cup semisweet chocolate morsels
- 1 tbsp coffee granules
- 2 tbsp whipping cream
- 1 tbsp butter
- 1 pound medium to large fresh strawberries (rinsed and patted dry)

Directions:

Line a baking sheet with parchment paper.

In a heat-resistant bowl, combine the chocolate morsels, coffee granules, whipping cream, and butter, and mix thoroughly.

Add 3" of water to a medium size pan, bring to a simmer over moderate heat. Turn the heat off, and place the bowl of chocolate-butter over the hot water, and melt. Stir the mixture until smooth.

Holding a strawberry by its stem and leaves, dip it carefully into the melted chocolate mixture. Shake off any excess and transfer to the prepared baking sheet. Repeat the process with the remaining strawberries.

Set aside to allow the chocolate to cool before transferring to the fridge for 20-30 minutes to set.

Coffee Custard Tart

If you are a fan of custard trust and can't wait for the first cup of coffee of the day, this coffee custard tart will tick all your boxes and then some!

Servings: 6-8

Total Time: 1hr 25mins

Ingredients:

Custard:

- 1½ cups strong French pressed dark roast coffee
- 7 egg yolks
- 2 cups heavy cream
- 2 tbsp sugar
- 2 tbsp all-purpose flour

Shortbread Crust:

- ½ cup unsalted butter
- ¼ cup turbinado sugar
- ½ cup all-purpose flour
- ½ cup whole wheat pastry flour
- A pinch of sugar

Directions:

First, prepare the coffee custard: Pour the French-pressed dark roast coffee into a small pan. Over moderate heat, simmer until reduced to around ½ cup. The stronger the coffee, the better the result.

In a second pan, whisk the egg yolks.

Whisk in the heavy cream, sugar, and ½ cup (less 1 tablespoon) of the concentrated coffee from Step 1. You will need the reserved coffee for the crust. Over low heat, and while stirring constantly, bring to a simmer. Cook until the mixture thickens and coats the back of a wooden spoon. The mixture will continue to thicken as it cools. Sieve the custard until it is lump-free, and put aside until needed to fill the crust.

For the shortbread crust: Preheat the main oven to 350 degrees F.

In an electric mixer bowl, cream the butter with the sugar.

Add the all-purpose flour and whole wheat pastry flour to the creamed mixture, and mix until combined. Next, stir in the concentrated coffee set aside earlier.

Transfer the dough to a 9" fluted tart pan and pat out until even.

Scatter a pinch of sugar evenly over the dough.

Using clean fingertips, press the crust into the pan and up its sides. Place a piece of parchment paper into the tart shell and fill it with baking beans.

Bake the crust in the preheated oven for 15 minutes.

Remove the crust from the oven, remove the paper and beans.

Return the crust to the oven and bake for another 10 minutes.

Remove from the oven, allow to cool slightly, and pour in the coffee custard from Step 3, spreading it out evenly using a rubber spatula.

Transfer to the fridge to chill.

Serve and enjoy.

Coffee Mousse Rice Pudding

The perfect after-dinner dessert or supper snack, this fluffy coffee-infused rice pudding will have everyone coming back for a second helping.

Servings: 8-10

Total Time: 20mins

Ingredients:

- 1 cup water
- 1 cup whole milk
- ⅓ cup sugar
- 1 cup jasmine rice
- 8 ounces cream cheese (softened)
- 1½ cups heavy whipping cream
- ⅓ cup confectioner's sugar
- ¼ cup brewed extra strong coffee

Directions:

In a pan, combine the water, milk, and sugar. Stir in the jasmine rice and cook over moderate heat for 18-20 minutes, until the rice is light and fluffy. Put aside to cool.

In the bowl of an electric mixer, process the cream cheese until soft.

Stir in the cream, and on high speed, mix until combined. While the mixer is running, one tablespoon at a time, add the confectioner's sugar.

Next, add the coffee and continue to mix until fluffy and combined, for around 3-5 minutes.

Transfer the rice pudding to the fridge for 30 minutes.

When you are ready to serve, fold the jasmine rice into the coffee cream and enjoy cold.

Dalgona-Style Cinnamon Coffee Brûlée

Break into the crisp caramelized topping and discover a decadent creamy coffee cinnamon custard. Enjoy!

Servings: 1

Total Time: 10mins

Ingredients:

- 2 tbsp coffee granules
- 2 tbsp sugar
- A pinch of cinnamon
- 2 tbsp hot water
- 8 ounces milk

Directions:

In a bowl, combine the coffee granules with sugar, cinnamon, and hot water and whisk for 5-7 minutes until fluffy and light.

Scoop the coffee froth over a glass of milk, and with a spoon, flatten the top.

Using a kitchen blow torch, lightly torch the froth to caramelize.

Date and Coffee Scones

Time for a break! Why not invite a few friends around for coffee and wow them with a batch of these warm date and coffee scones?

Servings: 10

Total Time: 25mins

Ingredients:

- Butter (to grease, as needed)
- ½ cup evaporated milk (warm)
- 1 tbsp 100% pure coffee granules
- ¼ cup granulated sugar
- 4 tsp baking powder
- 2 cups all-purpose flour
- ¼ tsp salt
- ⅓ cup butter (chilled and chopped)
- ½ cup dried dates (chopped)
- 1 tsp vanilla extract
- 1 tbsp granulated sugar

Directions:

Preheat the main oven to 425 degrees. Using butter, lightly grease a large cookie sheet.

In a small bowl, combine the evaporated milk with the pure coffee granules. Stir well to dissolve the coffee.

In a larger bowl, combine ¼ cup sugar together with baking powder, flour, and salt.

Using either two knives or a pastry blender, cut in the butter to a coarse crumb consistency.

Next, stir in the coffee mixture, dates, and vanilla to create a soft dough.

Knead the dough 5-6 times on a lightly floured, clean work surface. Pat the dough gently to a thickness of around ½".

With a cookie cutter, cut the dough into 2½ "circles and arrange in a single layer on the prepared cookie sheet.

Scatter 1 tablespoon of sugar over the tops and bake in the oven until browned lightly, for around 10-12 minutes.

Remove from the oven and serve warm.

Italian Prune Plums in Brandied Coffee Syrup

Italian prune plums, unlike the regular variety, aren't tart or sweet. Instead, they are moderately sweet and mellow tasting. And this is why they are perfect for desserts.

Servings: 4-6

Total Time: 8mins

Ingredients:

- 2 cups strong coffee
- 1 cup sugar
- 1 tsp vanilla extract
- 2 tbsp brandy
- 1¾-2 pounds Italian prune plums (halved and pitted)

Directions:

In a pan, combine the coffee, sugar, vanilla, brandy, and plums, and bring to a simmer. Cover with a lid, and simmer for 5-10 minutes, turning the plums over gently, a couple of times, until just tender.

Taste and sweeten with more sugar if needed to balance the flavor.

Serve the dessert, hot, warm, or chilled.

Mocha Cheesecake

Make the most of mocha and spoil yourself with a slice of this decadent cheesecake.

Servings: 8

Total Time: 3hrs 10mins

Ingredients:

- 8 ounces cream cheese (room temperature)
- ¼-⅓ cup granulated sugar
- 2 tsp coffee granules (dissolved in 1 tbsp hot water)
- 2 tsp vanilla extract
- 6 ounces semisweet chocolate morsels
- 1 cup heavy cream (whipped to stiff peaks)
- 1 (8") store-bought chocolate crust

Directions:

In a large mixer bowl, beat the cream cheese with the sugar, coffee, and vanilla until creamy.

Melt the chocolate morsels according to the package instructions. Add the melted morsels to the cream cheese mixture and mix until combined thoroughly.

Fold in the cream, and pour the mixture into the store-bought crust.

Transfer to the fridge until set, for a minimum of 3 hours.

Garnish with a dollop of additional whipped cream and enjoy.

Sweet Egg White Omelet with Chocolate Coffee Yogurt

If you are watching your weight but craving a sweet treat, try this yummy chocolate coffee egg white omelet. You won't be disappointed!

Servings: 1

Total Time: 8mins

Ingredients:

- ½ cup fat-free Greek yogurt
- 1 cup espresso coffee
- 1 tbsp unsweetened cocoa powder
- 1 tbsp water
- 8-10 drops liquid stevia extract (as needed)
- 1 cup egg white

Directions:

In a small bowl, combine the Greek yogurt, and espresso coffee, mixing to incorporate fully.

In another small bowl, combine the cocoa powder with water. Taste and sweeten if necessary with liquid sweetener.

In a bowl, combine the egg whites with the remaining liquid sweetener. Pour the mixture into a small omelet pan set over low heat. Cook the egg whites on one side, flip over and cook on the other side to create an omelet. When cooked, slide the omelet out of the pan.

Fill the omelet with the coffee yogurt, roll as you would a pancake, and drizzle with the chocolate sauce.

Author's Afterthoughts

I would like to express my deepest thanks to you, the reader, for making this investment in one my books. I cherish the thought of bringing the love of cooking into your home.

With so much choice out there, I am grateful you decided to Purch this book and read it from beginning to end.

Please let me know by submitting an Amazon review if you enjoyed this book and found it contained valuable information to help you in your culinary endeavors. Please take a few minutes to express your opinion freely and honestly. This will help others make an informed decision on purchasing and provide me with valuable feedback.

Thank you for taking the time to review!

Christina Tosch

About the Author

Christina Tosch is a successful chef and renowned cookbook author from Long Grove, Illinois. She majored in Liberal Arts at Trinity International University and decided to pursue her passion of cooking when she applied to the world renowned Le Cordon Bleu culinary school in Paris, France. The school was lucky to recognize the immense talent of this chef and she excelled in her courses, particularly Haute Cuisine. This skill was recognized and rewarded by several highly regarded Chicago restaurants, where she was offered the prestigious position of head chef.

Christina and her family live in a spacious home in the Chicago area and she loves to grow her own vegetables and herbs in the garden she lovingly cultivates on her sprawling estate. Her and her husband have two beautiful children, 3 cats, 2 dogs and a parakeet they call Jasper. When Christina is not hard at work creating beautiful meals for Chicago's elite, she is hard at work writing engaging e-books of which she has sold over 1500.

Make sure to keep an eye out for her latest books that offer helpful tips, clear instructions and witty anecdotes that will bring a smile to your face as you read!

Printed in Great Britain
by Amazon